LOVE LETTERS OF A WORSHIPPER:

Prayers, Poetry and Prose

Jadora's Child Publishing

Middletown, Connecticut

Dedication

This book is dedicated to my Grandmother, Eula Lee Fuller.
She was a fierce Woman of God and her example is one I still try to
live up to even today.
I miss you so much Nana! I love you! Thank you for teaching me about
Jesus! I love Him because of you.

Copyright © 2015 Liela Marie Fuller

Cover Design: MERK Media
Cover Image: © Fergregory | Dreamstime.com

ISBN- 0-9961289-4-8
ISBN-13: 978-0-9961289-4-0

Unless otherwise noted Scripture quotations are from The Holy Bible, King James Version.

ACKNOWLEDGEMENTS

I would like to thank God — my Heavenly Father. Getting to know you more has been the best thing I've ever done. I am your Princess because you told me that I am! Thank you Father God!

To my Lord & Savior Jesus Christ – thank you for dying on the cross for my sins! Thank you for taking on all of our sins so that we might have a chance to get it right!

Bishop-Elect Steven Hodge and First Lady Shirleen Hodge – thank you for everything. You are the best spiritual parents anyone could ask for. I am glad that God placed me in your loving care.

For my parents — thank you for all of your support. I love you.

For my Sissies — thank you for your love and your prayers. I appreciate you more every day. I thank God for you!

For Malachi — I love you son! You are great and mighty; I cannot wait to see God's promises fulfilled in your life.

TABLE OF CONTENTS

SANCTIFY THIS PLACE

Sanctify this place oh Lord

Anoint this place Lord

Show me your face today Lord

I want to go to another level and experience more of you, Lord.

I want to exist in the space where your face meets my worship where my heart leaps and speaks to you.

I want to take the next step in worship and present myself a living sacrifice, holy and acceptable to you.

Take me to another level in you, oh Lord!

Anoint my hands God and let them be instruments to glorify you.

Anoint my mouth God and let it speak the words of worship to you my God.

Open my heart and pour in more of you, Lord.

Open my mind and let my thoughts be your thoughts.

Move in me, God

Fill me with you, Lord.

I need more of you, oh Lord!

This intimacy we share — I need more of it.

This love we share — I need more of it.

Lord, take me to another level.

Let me feel your presence every moment, every second God.

Sweep across this place and breathe on me

Let me hear your voice and draw me into your embrace.

Lord, I need you

Lord, you are my everything.

Lord, I believe in you.

Lord, I trust you with all I am and all that I have.

Lord, take me to another level

Sweep this place and show me your face.

Let me be closer to you.

GET CLOSER TO ME

"Get closer and you will see... Get close, so close that there is no room, so not even air can get through." ~ My interpretation of what the Lord said to me.

Get closer

Much closer

Get closer

Despite what the days seem like around you

No matter what the night tries to tell you — get closer.

Don't run away into the pitch black

Stop believing He doesn't see

He sees it all — even your pain and He's longing for you to get closer.

He is concerned about everything great and small.

He truly hears it all.

He is concerned because He loves you.

He sees your tears

He hears your laugh

He even feels your pain

He knows every emotion after all He made them

So don't be ashamed to get close.

Despite what you've been told

Despite what you may see, God is always here for you and me.

We just have to get close — closer — much, much closer.

LORD, LET ME LOVE YOU THROUGH YOUR HEARTSTRINGS...

If it were up to me, Lord, in my humanity, I would not choose to walk this path.

If it were up to me, Lord, I am not sure I could, but you said, "Love your enemies, do good to them that spitefully use you"

But Lord, if it were really up to me, I'm not sure I could.

So, Lord Help me to love through your heartstrings.

Help me to do unto others as you said I should.

Lord, Help me to not to treat people like they treat me, but help me to treat them as you would — with Love and compassion.

Lord, you said that the greatest commandment is to Love.

You didn't give conditions on it...

You didn't say only love if they look like you, or talk like you...

You didn't say only love if they are poor or are rich...

You didn't say only love if they believe like you...

Your command was to Love yet Lord, in my humanity I find myself loving with conditions

So, Lord, help me to love through your heartstrings.

Lord, when someone has offended me and I am angry

When someone has mistreated me and my mind thinks of revenge.

Lord, when it is hard for me to love people because of the terror they inflict on me, Lord, Help me Love through your heartstrings.

When I've been abused and want to get even

When I've been tormented by people whose sole goal is to destroy
me
Lord, it's at these times when I need to love how you love.

Tell me, Lord, how did you still manage to forgive those who betrayed
you?
How did you still manage to Love them?
I want to love like that Lord — even when people try to destroy me, I
don't want to let that stop me from loving them like you love me.

Lord, let me love through your heartstrings...
Let me love your people the way you do...
Lord, I am so flawed and at times so broken and if I were really real I
couldn't love some people but I know that if you let me love through
your heartstrings I can love through anything.

I can love and forgive those who abandoned me
I can love and forgive those who didn't believe me
If I love through your heartstrings, Lord, then I can love them not for
who they are or what they did, but I can love them simply through
your heartstrings.

YES, YOU ARE

Lord, you are my banner.

Lord, you are my strong tower.

You are my provider.

Thank you for being my help Father.

Thank you for being my source.

Truly, you are my life and living in you is so good.

I want no other choice but to live my life with you.

Lord, I am stuck in your presence.

Your Glory fills this place and it overtakes me.

And I bow to worship you.

Lord, I could stay right here, in fact, there really is nowhere else I'd
rather be

Then here in the midst of worship with you.

It's not about what you will do or what you have done, but it's simply
about worshipping you for who you are.

You are my Lord and I love you for who you are.

THANK YOU

I was ready to give up and you prayed for me.

I was about to let go and drift away willing, to drown in my own sorrow and frustration.

Then God sent you my way to pray that I'd hold on a little while longer.

I was overwhelmed by life and circumstances.

I didn't feel like I even had the words to say, but God told you to pray!

What I realized in this walk with Christ is that we are never alone and sometimes when the weight is too heavy and we can't pray for ourselves, God sends someone along who can pray for us.

Thank you for Praying!

Thank you for loving me enough to pray.

You may not have known the circumstance, but God gave you an assignment and I am proof that prayer works.

And as you pray for me, know that I pray for you.

More and more I believe that in this manner we are our brother's keeper.

The song says, "I pray for you ~ you pray for me. I love you. I need you to survive." Those words take on new meaning for me because when God puts you on my heart, I know that my assignment is to pray. I don't need to know the details or the circumstances, it's not my business because my assignment is to pray.

James 5:16 Amplified says, "Confess to one another therefore your faults (your slips, your false steps, your offenses, your sins) and pray [also] for one another, that you may be healed and restored [to a spiritual tone of mind and heart]. The earnest (heartfelt, continued) prayer of a righteous man makes tremendous power available [dynamic in its working]."

So when you, the righteous pray, God not only hears you, but your prayer is making something happen. Your prayer is causing a shift in the atmosphere. Your prayer is causing God to move. Your prayer is causing God to work things out on their behalf. So don't ever think your prayer isn't working. Don't ever think your prayer isn't heard. God hears the prayers of the righteous and according to His Word — the earnest prayer of a righteous man makes tremendous power available. Let's keep praying for one another!

Thank you Lord for the power of prayer.

Thank you Lord for the words to pray and Thank you Lord that you hear our prayers.

I Will Worship You (I'm a True Worshipper)

Oh, Lord How I thank you.

How I adore you.

You loved me when I didn't love myself

You cared for me when no one else did.

You pulled me up from the miry clay

And Lord each and every day, I will worship you

Each day I'll kneel before you, hands lifted up, heart surrendered and submitted.

Loving You to Praising You to Worshipping You

Lord in that moment, it's like there is no one else in the room and no one else in the world — it's just me worshipping you.

Lord, I was built to worship you.

I was made to worship you.

If people were to look at the blueprint design of my life, they'd see worship written all over me.

Just like blood runs through my veins, worship is an instrumental part of me — it is a necessity.

Lord, it's not even, about what you do for me.

Abba, if you did nothing else I would still worship you.

I would worship you with nothing but the breath that is in my body

And if all I had left was one breath, I would worship you with it.

Lord, sometimes I get in your presence, I lose myself, and "I don't want to leave this holy place. I don't want to miss the miss the smile on your face."

Lord, all I want is to be in your presence forever.

All I want is to worship you.

God, my heart beats to the drum of worship for you!

I gave up the tradition of religion for a relationship with you

And oh, how beautiful it is to be close to you.

Lord, whatever is going on in my life, in worship I find an exchange.

As I enter into worship, I lay down everything that has taken up space in my mind and I cast my cares onto you Lord and as I do, not only am I free to worship, but you're taking my issues and you begin to work them out in the midst of my worship.

I leave our worship experience with wisdom and insight, but even more important a renewed passion to worship you.

I used to wonder what heaven would be like.

I used to wonder what we would all day, but now I know and it excites me!

I am excited to worship you freely in Heaven and in Earth.

We are built to worship the Lord in spirit and in truth, so worship is what we will do.

It's what the angels do.

Worship is my gift.

It is who I am.

It is an essential part of me.

It is the key to a relationship I am unworthy to have but God loves me more than enough to call me into relationship with him and I will worship Him with all that I have.

I'm not worthy to worship you Lord and I could never do anything to be worthy of your presence God but you love me anyway.
I came to this world unworthy, yet you still loved me, still sought me out, and still called for me to build a relationship with you and "Here I am to worship. Here I am to bow down. Here I am to say that you're my God. You're all together lovely; all together holy; all together wonderful to me."

Lord, all I ever want to do is worship you.
I could spend my days at the altar of your feet in worship.
I could spend my days worshipping you.
Some days I get so busy and there are so many things to do, that I feel empty because I need the opportunity to worship you.
I need the opportunity to be in your presence.
I need the opportunity to fall in worship and see your face.
I need the opportunity to open the door and lay before you — no distractions, no interference, Lord just me lying prostrate before you in true worship.
I am a worshipper Lord and I will spend my forever days worshipping you.

GOD CAN HAVE EVERYTHING I HAVE

(Dedicated to my Future Husband — thank you for the inspiration.)

He's got cattle on a thousand hills
And He can still have everything that I have

He gives me the power to get wealth, but I would give it all back in an instant if He asked me to.

God can have everything that I have sounded like a cute catchphrase, but then I met Him.
And when I began to know Him that catchphrase became my life.

God can have everything I have because I know that I can trust Him and He knows He can trust me.
If He says give up your car, there is probably a better car waiting for me.
If He says give up the house, He has a better one in the wings.
If He says leave the job, I'm confident He will sustain me.

What I have come to understand is that this stuff is only temporary and only what you do for Christ will last.
So yeah, God really can have everything I have — He can have all that I have.
Enjoying life with Him is more vital than the house, the car and the

money.

If the lesson is to live without all of that so I can get close to Him —
sign me up.
Would it be hard — yes — but the truth is that Heaven and earth will
pass away, because only what you do for Christ will last.

God can have everything I have because the gifts I've been given all
come from Him.
He's made me fearfully and wonderfully.
I owe Him my life, my gifts, and all I can do is surrender.

God can have everything I have. I may not understand it at the time
but the lesson is faith and trust, I don't always need to understand it.

My faith believes Him.
My heart loves Him
I worship Him with all that I am and all that I have.
God is my everything and He can have everything that I have.

LORD, WHAT I NEED IS UNDERSTANDING

Lord, help me when I don't feel like I'm good enough.

Help me when I'm overwhelmed by all the good you tell me.

Help me to know I'm worthy of it because you said I am.

Help me to know that my actions haven't made me worthy, but

because your word said so, I can have what you say I can have.

Even when it looks impossible… Even when it seems crazy… Even

when what you've said makes no natural sense, help me to receive

the blessings and help me not to be afraid of what I see just because

it's so much bigger than me.

Lord, help me to trust in your plan — a plan for my good and one that

many won't understand.

Help me to trust you, both in good and in bad because it all works

together…

Lord, help me to really understand.

RESOLUTE

I am resolute in my prayer like the resolute desk — I can't and won't be moved until you do it.

I am determined to stand in my faith until you move.

I am beyond the shouting and the tears because Lord I need your ear.

I'm seeking and I won't stop until I find you.

I am knocking and I won't stop until you answer.

I am unwavering in my resolve that you will do it — you have to!

If you don't, it won't happen.

I am resolute in my prayer like the President's desk — I am immovable.

I am resolute in my belief that you'll bless me and like Jacob, I won't stop until you do it.

I am resolute in my knowing that you are all I need and no devil in hell can have me — I am yours.

I believe you Lord, there is no wavering attack. No doubt or demands — just my resolute faith placed where it should be — in you!

There is no worry here Lord, just my purposeful prayers to you asking you to bless your people!

There is no fear that you won't because I am confident that you will.

Healing is the children's bread and I am your child so I am taking what I need — not more than enough, but what I need to be healed, whole, restored and delivered.

I am standing firmly planted with the root of your Word, knowing that if I saturate my life with your Word, I will be changed.

I need more than the facade the world gives — I need you Lord.

No more phony Christianity

No more dilly dally

No more towing the line — no more

I am determined that I want you Lord

I am determined that I want all that you have for me.

I am determined that I will be everything you have called me to be.

Sickness won't stop me.

Doubt won't stop me.

Fear won't stop me.

Friends won't stop me.

I am going after you like a hungry dog chases its food and I won't stop until you bless me!

I won't stop until you move in me.

I won't stop until you change me.

I won't stop until you fill me.

I won't stop until there is less of me and more of you.

I won't stop until I look more like you and less like me.

I am resolute in my stance, resolute in my prayer.

Lord, I am not moving, not one hour until you bless me! I am immovable waiting for you.

I am resolute.

Words In The Word

What if when we spoke things were created?

> *"In the beginning was the Word, and the Word was with God,*
> *and the Word was God. The same was in the beginning with*
> *God. All things were made by him; and without him was not*
> *anything made that was made."*
> *(Genesis 1:1-3)*

What if when you spoke life, it happened?

> *"And when he thus had spoken, he cried with a loud voice,*
> *Lazarus, come forth. And he that was dead came forth…"*
> *(John 11:43-44a)*

What if when we spoke death, it actually occurred?

> *"And when he saw a fig tree in the way, he came to it, and*
> *found nothing thereon, but leaves only, and said unto it, Let no*
> *fruit grow on thee henceforward forever. And presently the fig*
> *tree withered away." (Matthew 21:19)*

What if our words caused fear, frustration, anger, pain, heartache and doubt?

> *"Death and life are in the power of the tongue: and they that*
> *love it shall eat the fruit thereof." (Proverbs 18:21)*

What if, with our declarative words, we created peace, blessings, joy?

> *"Thou shalt also decree a thing, and it shall be established unto*
> *thee: and the light shall shine upon thy ways" (Job 22:28)*

Our words have the power to build up or tear down.

Our words have the power to edify or mislead

Our words have the power to showcase our Savior in worship or

18

spew hate for one another out of fear.

Ever notice when you say, "I'm tired," you become more tired?

Ever notice when you say, "I'm hungry," you become hungrier?

Just like the law of gravity, your words have power.

If we say, I'm poor

    Being poor is what we will be.

If we say, I'm rich

    Wealth and riches will be in our homes.

You will have just what you say every time because out of the heart the mouth speaks.

Death and life are in the power of the tongue so how are you using your words?

LORD REMIND ME

Help me not to feel overwhelmed by the pressures of work and all of the things that don't go my way.

Instead, Lord, remind me to be thankful and grateful for all that, you have so graciously provided.

Some days it's hard to go back into the woes of the world and leave the presence of our time in worship.

Even though I know you're always with me, there is a sound in Worship that is hard to hear when the world is turned on and the day begins its hustle and bustle.

There is a flow in worship where I can just bow, lay or kneel before you and when I step out into the world that sometimes gets dimmed.

Some days it's hard to leave because being in your presence is like air for my lungs; it's like water to my unquenchable thirst.

Being in your presence frees me and I can be surrounded by your glory.

I can lay at your feet uninterrupted by the noise of atmosphere.

In worship, it's just you and me, Lord, and I just want to stay right there — worshipping you.

Yet, when the alarm goes off it brings with it the noise of the world, the clanking calamity and the frustrations of life and I am like a child not wanting to leave its mother.

I cry not wanting to leave yet knowing you are always with me.

LIVE THROUGH ME

Lord, use me

I am your vessel, pour into me and use me for your glory.

Lord, speak through me

I am your mouthpiece

Let your words flow from my lips like water flows downstream.

Lord, live through these hands of clay

Lord, live through these feet

Let me walk and run wherever you send me sharing your love with the world.

Lord, live through this body that I dedicate to your service.

Lord, live through me

Anoint me freshly and pour your love into me.

Let my heart love like you love.

Let my thoughts be like your thoughts

And Let my mind be more like your mind.

Consecrate me, Lord.

Live through me, Lord.

Live through me.

LORD, BE THE ANSWER

When my mind is full of questions, Lord be the answer.

When I don't know what to do, Lord be the answer.

When I have lost all direction, Lord, provide me with instructions.

When I have lost my way, Lord be my compass.

When I'm hurt and confused, Lord, be the loving and unadulterated truth.

When the world has taken its toll upon me, Lord, be my refuge.

When the pain inside of me is overwhelming and overbearing, Lord heal me.

When life seems like its flying by, Lord be my respite.

When I am tired, Lord, be my strength and my ever-present help.

Lord, be the answer to ever prayer uttered.

Be the answer for every person on the brink of a breakthrough.

Be the answer for those seeking asylum in your bosom.

Be the answer to those seeking comfort at your feet.

Lord, we just need you to be the answer.

He Did It Just For Me

He did it just for me

The stripes he took them to set me free

Free from the bondage of sin; free to live again.

He took the beatings one after another so that I could stand free
from the wages of my sin.

He was born to die so that I might live

He took the stripes so that I might be healed.

As he fell and was beaten, he remembered me.

As he rose from the fall because of the weight of his cross, he
thought of me.

He knew that I needed him and so would you, so he rose from the
ground and took up his cross.

As he held up his cross, he bore the weight of my burdens and my
sins.

He knew that I'd sin before I was even born

Yet he became the slaughtered so that I might choose to live his way
someday.

I live today because he bore the death meant for me.

I live today because he bled on the way.

I live today because of the pain he endured.

On the way, he saw me and he knew he had to do it – he had to die
for me.

It should have been me who bore the stripes.

It should have been me to carry the cross.

It should have been me to have the nails driven into my hands.

It should have been me not Him, I am guilty and He is innocent.

Yet his love endured enough to take my place.

It should have been my blood to splash on the ground.

He endured the pain so that I might have more life and less pain.

It should have been me hung on the tree and died for my pride.

It should have been me who was nailed to the wood because I lied.

It should have been my side that was pierced for all of my sins.

Yet He bore it all for me, He bore everything, He bore it all for me.

ON THE MOUNTAINTOP

Lord, you met me on a mountaintop and you talked to me.

Lord, you met me on a mountaintop and as I prayed, you changed me.

I came to this mountain full of fears, worries, doubts and concerns trying to trust you but not fully handing things over.

I was caught between control and letting go.

I knew if I let go, you'd take all of my worries, my doubts, and my fears and fix them but I still needed to have control.

How would it look because I am always in control (or so I think).

I've always got it together (or so I let people believe).

I can't give up control (or at least I think I can't).

Giving up control looks too much like surrender and I can't surrender because I need to have control.

Yet, in my desire to be in control, I was surrendering to my fears.

I was surrendering to doubt every time I turned around to check my bank account to see if I could give an offering this week instead of trusting in your word completely.

I was surrendering to my worries every time I watched the movie the enemy played in my head of me losing everything, of my son damaged and bruised, of being alone forever.

And as I sat on the mountaintop, Lord, you said lay prostrate before me and as I did, you told me that there was nothing to fear.

You told me that you had me in the palm of your hand.

25

You told me to rest in your love.

You said that you make me to lie down in green pastures and you lead me beside the still waters.

Lord, you told me that you would restore my soul.

You told me that you would keep me if I would hold on and not let go.

I wept in your presence and I chose not to let go of your hands.

And in doing so, I willingly released my fear, my doubt, my worries and my concerns.

In doing so, I willingly surrendered.

I released my fear, my doubt, my worries and my concerns.

As I boarded the bus to leave the mountain top, no one knew the gravity of my experience with you but I know we all had an exchange.

No one really knew that I was exchanging my hurt for joy.

I was exchanging my fears for trust and obedience.

I was exchanging my worries for faith and favor.

I was exchanging my loneliness for what you had already told me was mine, if I just believed. And as I left my cares on the mountain and embraced your word and your will, I left the mountain changed.

I left the mountain ready, eager, willing, excited, but most importantly no longer in control.

I surrendered control over to you I know longer need it.

I surrendered it all to you Lord.

Now the weight of the issues are no longer mine, they belong to you.

You paid the price for me.

You give me favor and you restored me.

Thank you for meeting me on the mountaintop, thank you for taking my burdens....

THE STORM

As I stand, the storm beats against me.

Yet, I know who I am and in whom I trust and believe

So, I know that this too shall pass.

As I struggle to get free of the bonds that chain me

I see Him coming to release me because His Word says, "He shall

deliver me" and "He shall hide me in the shadow."

He shall hold me in the palm of His hand.

This storm will not destroy me.

This storm will make me stronger, wiser and better because I know

who I am.

I am a child of the King.

And no enemy can defeat me as long as He is with me.

No storm can overtake me because I am safe in His arms.

WHEN IT'S HARD TO BELIEVE

Sometimes I feel like I go through by myself.

Sometimes it feels like I carry the burden and weight of my issues and there is no one I can talk to who will believe for me.

When I called my Mom, she talked and complained about her issues. She just mumbled on and on as if upon my shoulders there was no weight to bear.

I called my best friend and while she asked me how I was doing and I believed she sincerely wanted to know, I knew her reply would be a carnal one and that's just no longer flies in my life.

So I thought long and hard about who I could turn to and the truth be told there was only one real answer.

So I took a moment and got rid of all the distractions, I closed the door and stopped listening to the world so that I could hear Him fully.

I sat on my bed and I prayed.

Just a conversation with the one who knows me best; had some things on my heart that people couldn't understand and since He was the one who created me, I knew He'd relate better to me.

Why I didn't come to this conclusion at the onset is beyond the scope of my recollection, but I know now there is no objection.

When I'm thankful, He's my first stop.

When I'm scared, He's truly my rock.

When I'm confused, He's always the answer.

When good things happen, I'm at His door shouting Thank you Lord because I couldn't have done it without Him.

Through every situation, what I've learned is that right or wrong, people may fail you, but God never ever will.

As much as I love my family and my friends, know that when I get
quiet, it's simply because my life depends on Jesus.

He is the solid rock that I stand on.

Lord, You are more

You are more than the pain in my heart

You are more than the sufferings I have endured.

You are more than the aches I have had in my soul.

It's you Father, who can heal me.

It's you Father who can restore me.

I don't need anything but Jesus.

Jesus you are more; Lord you are all that I've been looking for.

I've tried to find the answer in so many things, yet none ever satisfied me.

Those things could never fill the gap

They could not replace the pain.

Then I found you, and you loved me, Lord.

You filled the void and poured in your joy.

You healed the pain and erased every stain.

You were more than my circumstance and more than my shame.

More than my guilt and you erased all of my pain.

I needed your love to soothe the ache.

I needed your love to wash the tears away.

You are more Lord

More than any pain

More than my shame

More than every circumstance.

You, oh Lord, are more.

You, my Lord, are all that I need.

I LOVE YOU TO LIFE

Love is the key to life and it's what we need

I love you to life with all of me.

I love you with all of me — I love you to life and that's what I mean.

There is no day that I am not thankful for your grace

There is no day that I forget where you brought me.

Your love, Lord, gives me life and I love you to life.

Thank you Lord for your love; it envelops me, covers me and keeps me.

Lord, your love is amazing and so I have no choice but to love you to life with all of my life.

WHAT IF

What if every time I got angry, you received a lash?

What if every time I got uptight and paid others no mine, they whipped you?

What if my every action produced a reaction for you?

What then would I do?

Would I change how I respond or would I not even care about you?

What if my life was dependent on choosing you?

What if when you died, you made sure I didn't have to?

What if all of this was true?

Your love sent you to Calvary to stand in proxy for me!

You took my every sin on you and you chose to take my place

Not letting me die full of sin, but you took my place and let me live.

It should have been me hanging on that cross, but you took the burden for me.

So my sins are forgiven and I can live.

I can be forgiven for my anger.

I can be forgiven for my selfishness

I can choose you and live forever

Lord, you are amazing and without you, I am nothing.

Lord, you are my everything and without you I am less than

Lord, you are my cup and you run over in me.

Lord, you are my joy and my restoring measure.

Lord, I am unworthy of your love, but I thank you for stretching your arms wide and giving your life to love me.

THIRTY - THREE

Lord, as I reflect on what you did for me, I'm thankful.

Thankful that you left Heaven made yourself like me and lived.

You lived among the flowers and the trees the Father spoke into existence.

You ate the fish he called into the sea.

You healed the bodies that carried the breath God breathed into Adam.

You lived!

You walked among us - a King

Serving others

Delivering others

It was you Lord

33 years of walking among us, allowing those among you to glean from you, learn from you and love you.

Then one day the fullness of your purpose on this earth became clear - you came not to live, but to die so that we could live.

You put on a suit of humanity for us.

You felt pain for us.

You endured shame for us.

You were bruised for us.

You were beaten for us.

You hung on a tree for us.

And had you been any other man the story would have ended there
But, you aren't any other man ~ you are Jesus!
While everyone thought you were gone, you conquered death, hell
and the grave and when they returned, they found you not there but
arose out of the grave.
Because you are not just an ordinary man
You are Jesus.

You didn't stay dead
You rose
You changed the course of history
You changed the course of my life
You see, you took the beatings meant for me
You took the death, I should have endured
All because you loved me

Thank you Lord for loving me

PERFECTED PRAISE / WONDROUS WORSHIP

Praise is what I do

A Worshipper is who I am

Praise is what I say

Worship is what gets me through the day

Praise is outstanding

Worship is necessary

Praise is for a purpose

I Worship because I love you.

Worship takes me to your feet

Praise takes me to the door of your sanctuary and it knocks on my behalf

Worship gets me through the door and into your presence

Worship leaves me open to your will — vulnerable to you.

Worships cracks open my hard shell and your love come flying through

Worship gets me to the place where it's no one but you and me.

Worship takes me to your feet

My posture in worship is rarely up; it's always down ~ laying prostrate before you.

Oh, how I long for our times together ~ me worshipping you.

Worship rejuvenates my heart, my mind, and my spirit.

Being in your presence changes me.

Hearing your voice and feeling your loving embrace makes me not want to leave this place.

I'd rather be here with you than almost anywhere.

There is no place greater — truly worshipping at your feet is the greatest place on earth and in Heaven.

If I could stay for days in your presence, I certainly would.

I could lay prostrate before you day in and day out.

I look forward to the encounters in worship and I believe that the best things happen in worship and in your presence.

Worshipping You Gets Me Through

When I am frustrated and confused, worshipping you brings me closer to you.

When I put my eyes on you - the world seems less crazy and all the issues begin to fade. And life takes a back seat because being with you is better than anything.

When I am unsure and not confident in me, worship brings me right to your feet where your love replaces my fears, renews my strength and reassures me that I am your princess.

When the pain of loss overwhelms me, I worship you and your love overtakes me.

When the day -to -day burdens of my life try to bombard me, I know that I can take a moment to lay it all down and worship you.

Worshipping you gets me through everything - from the small challenges to giant trials because it brings me closer to you.

I can hear you speak.

I can feel your presence.

I can get help for my trials.

I get to replace my sorrow with your joy.

Worship gets me through the bad and the good.

Worship is sometimes all I want to do.

Make Me Over

Lord,

I need a makeover, not one from head to toe, but one from soul to spirit.

Lord, make me over

Lord, I need you to rid me of my fears, purge me of my false desires and make my heart like yours.

Lord, please, make me over

I packed up all of my emotional baggage and I need an exchange of these rags for riches.

I need space in this place to be used by you.

Lord, please make me over.

I don't want to live like this anymore; I'm tired of being broke and broken.

I'm tired of being sad, depressed, angry, frustrated and confused.

I know that I don't have to live like that when I am with you

Lord,

Sometimes I feel inadequate and less than

I feel like the burdens of my life are just much too much to bear

Sometimes I feel like the weight of what you said is too overwhelming for me

Sometimes I'd rather be nothing than to be what you see - it's not because it isn't great, but simply because, for me, it's so hard to believe

Help me to leave these weights and doubts at the altar with you.

Lord, remind me that the promises you have given are true

Remind me that all you have said is never too much.

FROM THE AUTHOR

Thank you for taking this journey through my Love Letters to the Lord. I pray that you were blessed, moved and that through my Love Letters you have drawn closer to God. It is my esteemed honor to have you read this book, but I understand that not everyone who reads it will know Jesus Christ and it would be my honor to introduce you today. If you don't know Jesus, would you take a moment and pray this prayer?

PRAYER: God, I acknowledge that in my life I have not made all the right choices. I have sinned and fallen short of your glory and the purpose for my life. Today, God, I confess of my sins and I pray that you would forgive me. I believe that your son Jesus Christ died on the cross for me. Jesus took my place and today I pray that Jesus would come into my heart and be my Lord and Savior. God, I put my life in your hands for guidance and direction and I believe that you have the best intentions and purposes for my life. I submit my life to you Lord have your way. In Jesus name, Amen.

Now, if you prayed that prayer send me an email (lielamfuller@jadoraschild.com) and let me know because I would love to hear from you. Also, find a bible believing church in your area that can help to minister to you right where you are. I know God has great plans for you and I am excited about what God is about to do in you!

Liela

Upcoming Titles From Jadora's Child Publishing

Poured from a Broken Vessel

Shanean Paige Saylor

Girlfriend Prayers – Prayers for my Sister Friends

Liela Marie Fuller

Love Letters of a Worshipper – Volume 2

Liela Marie Fuller

Be sure to visit our website – www.jadoraschild.com - for more details and to follow all of our authors. Follow us on Facebook (https://www.facebook.com/jadoraschildpublishing) and Twitter (@authorljmarie)

About the Author

Liela Marie Fuller is an Author, Poet, and Founder of Jadora's Child Publishing. Over the years, she has written countless poems, short stories and articles on everything from love to politics. Her editorial writings have been published in the Hartford Courant newspaper.

Liela founded Jadora's Child Publishing in 2014 to help these writers become successful authors. In addition to being the founder and CEO of Jadora's Child Publishing, Liela is also working on three new books to be published in 2015. Liela is also the founder of Heavenly Help Computer Solutions and MERK Media.

Liela was born and raised in Camden, NJ and is the proud Mother of one son and Auntie of many nieces and nephews. Liela is also an avid reader, car enthusiast, and coffee connoisseur! When Liela is not writing, she enjoys spending quality time with family and friends.

www.ingramcontent.com/pod-product-compliance
Lightning Source LLC
Chambersburg PA
CBHW022341040426
42449CB00006B/658